UNSOLVED MYSTERIES

Crop Circles

ABDO
Publishing Company

Crop Circles

by Andrea Pelleschi

Content Consultant
Colin Andrews
Author, Researcher,
and Engineer

CREDITS

Published by ABDO Publishing Company, PO Box 398166
Minneapolis, MN 55439. Copyright © 2012 by Abdo Consulting
Group, Inc. International copyrights reserved in all countries.
No part of this book may be reproduced in any form without
written permission from the publisher. The Essential Library™ is a
trademark and logo of ABDO Publishing Company.

Printed in the United States of America,
North Mankato, Minnesota
102011
012012

Editor: Melissa York
Copy Editor: Kathryn-Ann Geis
Series design: Becky Daum, Christa Schneider, & Ellen Schofield
Cover production: Christa Schneider
Interior production: Christa Schneider & Becky Daum

Library of Congress Cataloging-in-Publication Data
Pelleschi, Andrea, 1962-
  Crop circles / by Andrea Pelleschi.
      p. cm. -- (Unsolved mysteries)
  Includes bibliographical references.
  ISBN 978-1-61783-300-7
  1. Crop circles. I. Title.
  AG243.P34 2012
  001.94--dc23
                          2011038209

Table of Contents

Chapter 1

Mysterious Discoveries

On July 31, 1999, croppies Werner Anderhub and Hans Peter Roth came to Wiltshire, England, to conduct an investigation. They rose before dawn that early summer morning, hoping to discover their own crop circle.

Since the late 1970s, Wiltshire County in southern England has been the focus of a phenomenon known as crop circles. During the summer season, these mysterious circles appear in fields of cereal crops, such as oats or wheat, flattening the grain into smooth circles or elaborate shapes. Some of the shapes are pictograms. Some are graphic representations of mathematic formulas. Some are so beautiful they are considered works of art. Unfortunately, the art is temporary. Crop circles emerge overnight without fanfare and disappear just as quietly when farmers eventually harvest their crops.

Wiltshire County has become famous for its many crop circles.

Wiltshire

Wiltshire County in southern England boasts some of the most beautiful landscapes in England. It sits on chalk uplands, which are composed of a type of limestone formed into hills. The area includes a grassy plain called the Marlborough Downs, heavy woods, clay vales, and a limestone ridge that is part of the Cotswold Hills.

During prehistoric times, Wiltshire was one of the most populated areas in England. Monuments and barrows from the Neolithic Period fill the countryside, the most famous of which is the giant stone circle of Stonehenge.

Along with another man, Anderhub and Roth drove down a rural road near Pewsey, a small village approximately 80 miles (129 km) west of London. They parked their car, pulled out night vision goggles, and began watching East Field, an area known for previous crop circles. Overhead, a crescent moon shone down on the stalks, while a shimmery mist floated just above the ground. It was bitterly cold. As they waited and watched, sheep bleated off in the distance.

After a short while, they decided to move on to Avebury, another area known for its crop circles. They parked their car and walked to the top of Avebury Hill, from which they could easily see the surrounding countryside. After pulling out their night vision goggles, they scanned the fields below them. Again, they waited and watched. And again, they saw nothing.

It was time to try a third location known for crop circles. As the group drove up the narrow, winding

AVEBURY: Dating to 2800 BCE, Avebury is an ancient stone structure called a megalith. It includes the largest henge, or stone circle, in the world, as well as Silbury Hill, the largest prehistoric mound in the world. Because ancient monuments and modern crop circles are both prevalent in southern England, some people draw connections between the two.

road to Roundway Hill Farm, the sky began to glow pink with the coming dawn. They parked at the top of a hill and surveyed the field. As it grew brighter outside, the men were able to make out a shape among the stalks of wheat. Pulling out their binoculars, they watched eagerly as the sun came up.

The shape was regular and geometric. It had to be a crop circle. More important, it was a new crop circle. They knew this because they had been surveying all of the fields in the area for the past

Night vision goggles amplify the existing light that is reflected off all objects. They are useful in all levels of light except complete darkness.

several days. According to the farmer, the field was empty the day before. Now it was not.

Surveying the Circle

After their discovery, the group approached the farmer at Roundway Hill Farm and asked his permission to enter the field and examine the crop circle. The farmer, Christopher Combe, readily agreed and took them down a tramline, or tractor track, that passed between tall stalks of wheat.

The crop circle was enormous and complicated. Rough measurements revealed it to be approximately 138 yards (125 m) in diameter. Though it was hard to see the details from ground level, they determined that it consisted of a large inner circle surrounded by seven pointed areas topped by smaller circles out beyond the points.

WHEAT: Wheat is type of food plant called a cereal grass. It has long, hollow stems topped by a group of flowers in a spikelet. There are thousands of varieties of wheat. The most common are the *Triticum aestivium*, used for baking bread, and the *Triticum durum*, used for making pasta.

Combe was astonished that such a thing could appear in his wheat without his knowledge. "This formation was not here yesterday evening—I know, because I was working in an

Ultralight aircraft are extremely lightweight planes with smaller engines than conventional aircraft. They are perfect for people who need to fly low to the ground at a slower speed.

adjoining field. If it was created by something other than human hands, I'm actually proud of that fact, that something like this has happened in my field, of all places."[1]

In order to see the entire crop circle, the men needed to fly over the farm. After obtaining Combe's permission—with the promise of a couple photographs of the formation—the group set out in an ultralight aircraft. The plane belonged to Graham Slater, a pilot who drew in a brisk business taking croppies over fields to look at crop circles. On a good day, he might be able to show as many as 20 different crop circles in the area. On that day, however, there was only one circle that everyone wanted to see.

From approximately 1,000 feet (300 m) in the air, Slater flew through the endless blue skies from Clench Commons, where he kept his plane, to Roundway Hill Farm. The crop circle was so large that the group could see it from several miles away. As they flew closer, they saw that it resembled a jester's cap or a couple of crowns placed back to back. For this reason, people began calling it "The Crown."

One of the group members described The Crown this way: "Because it glistens in the morning sun in various shadings, according to the direction you see it from, it has a stunning three-dimensional character. It is as though an immense piece of gold jewelry, such as a brooch, is lying in the countryside."[2]

"In 1996, a circle appeared near Stonehenge, and the farmer set up a booth and charged a fee. He collected £30,000 ($47,000) in four weeks."[3]

—John Lundberg, an admitted crop circle maker, talking about farmers in Wiltshire

Anderhub and Roth had indeed struck gold. They had discovered a new crop circle.

Features of a Crop Circle

Crop circles can range from simple circles in a field of grain to complicated pictograms or graphic representations of mathematical formulas. Yet they all share common features.

One of the most telling characteristics is how the stalks of grain are not broken. They are bent at a 90-degree angle, still alive. If a farmer allows the grain to continue growing, then the plants sprout parallel to the ground. Some experts believe this lack of damage to the stems indicates that the circles must have been created in a matter of seconds. Some people even claim to have seen circles formed in less than 15 seconds.

Another characteristic is how the grains are all bent in the same direction, usually spiraling from the center of the circle. Once in a while, the stalks are interwoven in a deliberate fashion, similar to a braid, but they never overlap randomly.

The edges of crop circles are sharp and clearly defined. They often follow the tramlines in the fields, and they usually fit within a single field of crops. Many believe this indicates that crop circles are designed consciously rather than created by a random event, such as a weather pattern.

The controversy surrounding crop

PICTOGRAMS: Pictograms are simple drawings that represent a physical object, an idea, or even a word. The first pictograms, such as paintings on cave walls, are thought to be the forerunner of modern writing.

circles, though, is not about what they look like. Rather, the controversy is concerned with how crop circles are formed. Some people look at these common characteristics as an indication that intelligent life, perhaps alien life, created all of the crop circles. Some believe they are caused by a mysterious manifestation of Earth's energy. Some blame unusual weather patterns. Others look at the same evidence and say that all circles are a hoax, created by humans. Until definitive proof becomes available, the mystery remains: What exactly are crop circles, and how are they formed?

Crop circles appear mysteriously in farmers' fields.

The investigations continue to this day as crop circles continue to appear all over the world. Croppies travel to the Wiltshire and other crop circle hot spots, hoping to find the answers to these questions or to see a crop circle for themselves.

CROPPIES: Croppies are people who are interested in crop circles. They often travel to Wiltshire during the summer months and stay in one of the local inns. Croppie tourists are important to the region's economy, and local businesses welcome them. The Barge Inn, located in Honeystreet, even serves a beer called the Croppie ale.

Chapter 2

Early Sightings

Even though most crop circles seem to have occurred in the latter part of the twentieth century, evidence suggests they may have been appearing for hundreds of years before then.

The First Circles

On August 22, 1678, the earliest instance of what might be a crop circle was recorded in a pamphlet entitled *Mowing Devil*. This paper told an outlandish tale of a farmer from Hertfordshire, England, looking for someone to help him harvest his crop of oats. When a harvester named a price the farmer thought too high, the farmer

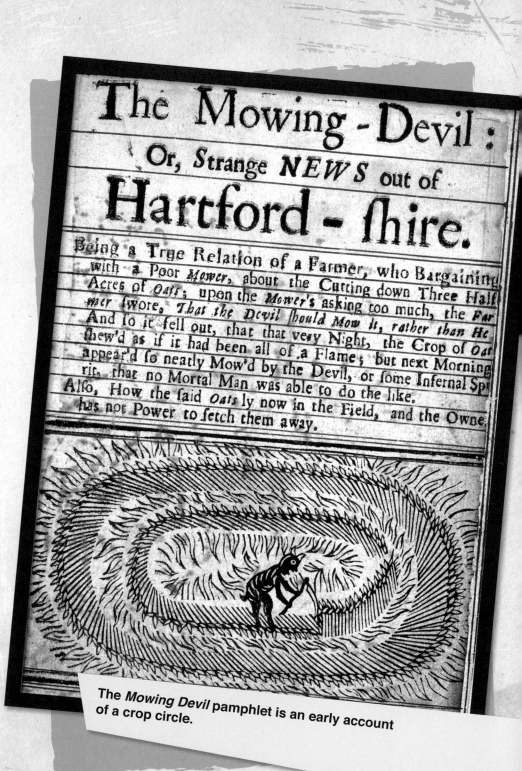

The Mowing - Devil :

Or, Strange NEWS out of

Hartford - ſhire.

Being a True Relation of a Farmer, who Bargaining with a Poor *Mower*, about the Cutting down Three Half Acres of *Oats*; upon the *Mower*'s asking too much, the Farmer ſwore, *That the Devil ſhould Mow it, rather than He.* And ſo it fell out, that that very Night, the Crop of Oat ſhew'd as if it had been all of a Flame; but next Morning appear'd ſo neatly Mow'd by the Devil, or ſome Infernal Spirit, that no Mortal Man was able to do the like. Alſo, How the ſaid *Oats* ly now in the Field, and the Owner has not Power to fetch them away.

The *Mowing Devil* pamphlet is an early account of a crop circle.

declared he would rather "the devil himself should mow his oats" than pay the harvester such a high price.[1]

That night, according to the pamphlet, the sky looked as though it were on fire. In the morning, the farmer discovered a precise circle had been cut into his field. A woodcut of the incident shows a devil forming what looks like a modern-day crop circle.

In 1880, a letter written by John Rand Capron appeared in the journal *Nature*, describing a mysterious circle he had observed in Surrey, England. "We found a field of standing wheat considerably knocked about, not as an entirety," said Capron, "but in patches, forming, as viewed from a distance, circular spots."[2] Capron went on to describe how the stalks had been swirled into perfectly round shapes, perhaps by a strong rain or wind. He hypothesized that a whirlwind or a cyclone may have caused the formation to occur.

NATURE: Established in 1869, *Nature* is a journal dedicated to presenting scientific findings to the general public as well as giving scientists a place to learn about new discoveries. Over the years, *Nature* has published articles on topics such as the first X-rays, the splitting of the atom, and the structure of DNA.

The Early Twentieth Century

During the 1920s through the 1930s, there is anecdotal evidence of crop circles appearing in southern England. Farmers tell stories of playing in them when they were young.

One story came from Roger Sear when he was a boy living in Sussex, England, in the 1920s. For years, Sear ventured into crop circles, or "witch's rings" as he called them. He reported experiencing some strange phenomena while inside the circles. His pocketknife became magnetized after he shoved it into the ground. His dog refused to enter the crop circle. The needle on his compass spun crazily while he was inside the circle, and, when he came out of it, the needle stopped pointing north. Instead, the needle pointed toward the circle.

In 1935, a ten-year-old boy from Essex, England, claimed to have seen a crop circle form right before his eyes. He said a whirlwind created the circle. An adult who was with the boy at the time was unimpressed, dismissing it

In a magnetic compass, a needle made of iron or steel is magnetized and allowed to rest on a pin on the bottom of the compass. This needle then spins toward Earth's magnetic North Pole.

as a "devil's twist" and claiming that crop circles like this one had been happening in southern England for at least a hundred years.[3] In 1943, the first photograph of a crop circle was taken by a member of the Royal Air Force (RAF) while he was flying over Sussex in southern England.

The Shift to Aliens

During the first half of the twentieth century, society transferred the blame for the mysterious circles from the devil or witches to aliens from other planets. One reason for this change was the rising popularity of science fiction. Themes such as space travel, time travel, utopian societies, and aliens, which had been introduced to the world in the late nineteenth century by writers such as H. G. Wells and Jules Verne, were now gripping the minds of the public.

In addition, the new study of rocket science was making the idea of space travel more likely. Two pioneers in rocket science were inspired by science fiction writers. Russian scientist Konstantin E. Tsiolkovsky loved Verne's work, while American scientist Robert H. Goddard was influenced by Wells's novel *The War of the Worlds*, in which aliens from Mars invade England. Both scientists worked to develop rocket engines in order to make travel through space a possibility.

By the late 1930s, the idea of danger coming from space became more believable to many. In fact, in 1938, many Americans were fooled into believing that aliens had invaded Earth when radio host Orson Welles read *The War of the Worlds* to his listening audience.

The 1970s

The first documented modern crop circle occurred on August 15, 1972, in England. Arthur

Aliens continue to capture the public's imagination into the twenty-first century, as in the 2005 remake of *War of the Worlds*.

Shuttlewood and Bryce Bond claimed to have witnessed a circle form while they were looking at a wheat field after dark. "The grain flattened like a lady's fan opening up," said Shuttlewood. "A perfect circle resulted in less than a minute, while a very high-pitched tone could be heard."[4] Bond described the circle as swirling in a counterclockwise direction, forming a shape that was triangular rather than circular. In addition to that formation, they discovered two other crop circles nearby: one was round and the other was shaped like a cigar.

Throughout the 1970s, crop circles continued to appear in southern England, sometimes alone and sometimes in small groupings. Often, reports of mysterious lights in the night sky preceded the circles, leading to speculation that alien spacecraft, or unidentified flying objects (UFOs), were somehow creating them.

UFOs

A UFO is defined as any unusual object or incident in the sky that is not recognized by observers. The first recorded modern-day UFO sighting took place in the state of Washington in 1947, when Kenneth Arnold, a businessman and pilot, was flying his small plane. He saw nine objects zoom past him at a high rate of speed and told the newspapers the objects moved like saucers, or dishes, skipping over water. Thinking that Arnold meant the objects were shaped like saucers, they mistakenly printed it that way in the papers. To this day, UFOs are also called flying saucers.

In 1978, in Hampshire, England, a more complicated grouping of crop circles occurred. Called a quintuple, it had a pattern consisting of one large circle in the middle with four smaller circles around it, evenly spaced. Some people thought the pattern of the circles looked like the feet of a NASA lunar landing craft, which reinforced the idea that UFOs were involved in the formation of crop circles.

The Phenomenon Takes Off

In 1981, retired electromechanical engineer Patrick Delgado heard about

NASA'S LUNAR MODULE: During the Apollo missions in the 1960s and 1970s, astronauts used a Command and Service Module to fly from Earth to the moon. Then they climbed into a smaller vehicle called the lunar module and used that to descend to the moon's surface. On the surface, the lunar module rested on four round footpads.

a new formation of crop circles in the valley at Cheesefoot Head near Winchester, England. The precise set of three circles—one large circle in the middle with two smaller ones flanking it—astounded him. Not only were the smaller circles exactly half the size of the large circle, they were precisely aligned along their center lines. Delgado tried to imagine what could have caused the phenomenon. There

Colin Andrews and Pat Delgado investigate a crop circle in 1989.

were no tramlines and no evidence of people walking to or from the crop circle. It appeared that whatever had made the circles had to have come from the air.

"They were the first circles I had ever seen at close range," he said, "and the impact they had on me was sensational."[5] So sensational, in fact, that Delgado told local newspapers about it, as well as the BBC and ITN, two large television networks. Though the local Wiltshire paper had previously reported on crop circles, Delgado's story brought crop circles to the attention of the rest of the world.

In July 1983, electrical engineer Colin Andrews had a similar experience. He was driving past an area in Hampshire called the Devil's Punchbowl, a wide hollow or valley. A group of people were standing on the side of the road looking out over the valley, so Andrews pulled over and joined them. What he saw left him stunned. A set of five circles had been pressed down into the crops. They looked as if they had been made by five large cookie cutters, except the crops were still there, flattened instead of cut. The largest circle was 17.5 yards (16 m) in diameter, and the four smaller circles were 4.5 yards (4 m) in diameter. It was a precise quintuple.

After that, Andrews and Delgado teamed up to systematically document everything they could

A NEW TERM: In the 1980s, Andrews coined the term *crop circle*. The term became an entry in the Oxford Dictionary in 1997.

about crop circles, becoming the first experts on the subject. They took measurements of the circles, recorded eyewitness accounts, and kept precise records. In 1985, amateur pilot and photographer Busty Taylor began flying them over fields so they could spot their own crop circles. With Taylor's aid, they took their first aerial photographs, and in 1989, they published the very first book on the subject, *Circular Evidence*.

Throughout the 1980s, the number of crop circles increased from a few dozen per year to more than 300 in 1989. The complexity increased as well. Initially, the formations were simple circles. Then they were combinations of two or three circles together. Over time,

MEASURING CROP CIRCLES: When the team of Delgado, Andrews, and Taylor investigated a crop circle on the ground, their equipment included a film camera, a tripod, a video camera mounted on a pole so it could be swung out over the circle, a compass to find magnetic north, a step ladder to take pictures from above, a 65-foot (20-m) tape measure, and a notepad and pencil.

quintuplets became regular sights, as did formations with single and double rings. These complicated designs often looked like diagrams of the solar system or of an atom.

The Early Theories

In 1980, Dr. Terence Meaden, a meteorologist and founding member of the Tornado and Storm Research Organization, hypothesized that whirlwinds caused the crop circles. He believed these spinning columns

PLASMA VORTICES: Plasma is any gas that can conduct electricity. A plasma vortex is a whirlwind of electrically charged air. The theory is that when a plasma vortex touches down on a field of crops, it electrocutes them. This causes the plants to form a circle or another pattern.

of air touched down and swirled the crops into the perfect circles that were appearing in England. This would be similar to how a tornado touches down, but on a less-destructive scale. As the formations became more complicated, he modified his theory to say that the whirlwinds, which he called "plasma vortices," were charged with electricity. However, none of his theories explained why the plants were flattened rather than torn out of the ground. Nor did they explain the more complicated combinations of circles and rings.

Operation White Crow

In 1989, Delgado and Andrews organized a massive surveillance operation to try to see a crop circle being formed. More than 60 scientists and support personnel descended on the Devil's Punchbowl, armed with infrared cameras, video cameras, and other detection equipment. They saw mysterious lights and heard some strange trilling sounds. Sound experts showed that this distinctive trilling sound was similar but not identical to a bird known as the grasshopper warbler. When no crop circle appeared, the operation concluded after approximately one week.

More logical explanations were hard to come by. In 1985, a British officer from the air base at Middle Wallop told Delgado that pilots had taken an interest in the crop circles and were photographing them from the air. He had studied the pictures and could not come up with a good explanation for their existence. A hoax seemed unlikely to him because there were no paths to or from the circles, so he filed a report with the UFO Investigation Desk of the Ministry of Defense in London.

Other theories ran the gamut from pranksters using hot air balloons to farmers spraying too much fertilizer in their fields, the military performing secret operations, or something supernatural or extraterrestrial sending a message. As the decade ended, the crop circle phenomenon had created more questions than answers.

Chapter 3

Complicated Designs

By 1990, crop circles had become famous, and the public was eager to figure out what these mysterious designs were all about. *Circular Evidence* was a best seller in the United Kingdom. As croppies flocked to southern England that spring, crop circle designs took another step in the evolution from simple circles to something else entirely.

The First Pictograms

On May 23, 1990, the first pictogram appeared in a field below Telegraph Hill, near Cheesefoot Head, England. This design had a thin centerline with barbell-like circles at either end. Four unconnected square shapes were also impressed into the field. The entire formation looked nothing like any of the crop circle designs that had come before, and when similar pictograms appeared in June, many people saw these new crop circles as proof that an intelligent life was creating them—either human hoaxers or extraterrestrial aliens. They no longer believed that whirlwinds were creating crop circles.

During this time, local residents near Silbury Hill set up an amateur surveillance operation to see if they could observe a crop circle as it formed. During ten days in June, as the residents kept watch during the night, they reported hearing strange noises and seeing mysterious lights over the fields. George Wingfield, an organizer of the event, said the lights "moved slowly and rather low above the stalks of the wheat field."[1] A similar light was spotted over Milk Hill, close to an existing crop circle formation.

The day after the lights were seen, tiny crop circles appeared in the fields, approximately 1.5 feet (.45 m) in diameter. The "grapeshots," as they were named,

SILBURY HILL: Silbury Hill is a 130-foot (40-m) chalk hill near Avebury that was built in 2200 BCE. Scientists have not determined the purpose of the mound, but some believe it was used to observe the surrounding area. The remains of a spiral staircase and a moat can still be seen on the hill.

had no path to or from them, and no obvious explanation existed as to how they were formed.

Crop Circle Research

In late 1985, Andrews, Delgado, and Taylor formed the first research organization created specifically to investigate crop circles, Circles Phenomenon Research International (CPRI). The organization amassed an enormous database of all things related to crop circles. For many years, the CPRI published a newsletter about crop circle phenomena.

In April 1990, another group of people interested in studying crop circles formed the Center for Crop Circle Studies (CCCS). Their goal was to bring together people of many different backgrounds and to approach crop circles free of bias.

More Complicated Pictograms

During the night on July 10 of that summer, residents in the valley of Pewsey reported hearing a humming noise coming from a field overlooking Adam's Grave, a Neolithic barrow. The next morning, many people had trouble starting their cars. A possible reason soon became clear: the most complicated crop circle to date had appeared overnight in the Pewsey field.

In this new type of pictogram, circles and rings were centered on an axis with additional offshoots that resembled the letters *E* or *F*. The entire image was approximately 550 feet (168 m) long. No one knew what the symbols meant. Some thought the markings were meteorological. Others thought the entire design represented a dragon.

When Delgado saw the crop circle, he was amazed. "Soon we saw the strangest pictogram we had ever seen in the field below us. The pattern is so complicated that an exact description would fill several pages. . . . Especially the key-shaped forms caught our attention because of their composition of squares and rectangles. . . . The difference from the pictograms of the former weeks, which were already very complex, was breathtaking."[2]

Pictogram photographed by Andrews, 1990

Additional pictograms continued to appear that summer, including a spiral-shaped diagram near Allington Down that resembled a giant snake curled up on the ground.

As photographs and news reports of this new type of crop circle spread throughout the world, people swarmed to southern England, trampling fields and inadvertently destroying the crop circles in their enthusiasm.

Operation Blackbird

Even though Operation White Crow of the previous year had turned up no hard evidence, Delgado and Andrews decided to try it again. With the aid of both the media and the military, they set up another surveillance operation at Bratton Castle in Wiltshire. The entire operation was supposed to last three weeks, from the end of July into mid-August. The BBC and Nippon Television sponsored the event, and the military lent sophisticated, high-definition cameras to the operation, as well as the personnel to operate them.

Two days after Operation Blackbird began, Andrews was notified that a crop circle had formed out on the field, complete with sightings of mysterious lights. Andrews and Delgado excitedly told the media about the new crop circle before they had a chance to investigate it themselves.

The next morning, with camera crews following behind and helicopters circling overhead, they walked into the circle and discovered that the crop circle was clearly man-made. The lines were uneven. The circle itself was not precise. And to top it off, a wooden crucifix and a board game had been set in the middle of the crop circle.

With the world watching, Andrews and Delgado admitted to the cameras that the crop circle was a hoax and the mysterious lights had probably been the flashlights of the hoaxers as they made the circle.

To this day, no one has claimed responsibility for the hoax, but many people believe the military might have been responsible, using the hoax to diffuse the excitement over the crop circle phenomenon. The fact that the military personnel were missing the night the crop circles appeared seems to support this assertion.

Bratton Castle is a hill fort that dates back to the Iron Age. It was excavated before 1775 and is one of Wiltshire's oldest archaeological digs. A remarkable drawing of a white horse decorates one side of the fort.

If the military were to blame, then its plan paid off. After the hoax, interest in crop circles waned, and the media became much more skeptical about the origins of crop circles.

Representing Life

The following year, the summer crop circle season started quietly. A handful of pictograms appeared that were similar to the 1990's formations. Then in July, crop circle season suddenly took off. A new crop circle appeared nearly every day, sometimes as many as seven a day. Many of these were not ordinary pictograms, though. They were designs that seemed to represent life forms on Earth.

Insect pictograms, called "insectograms," looked like spiders or beetles. Large, bulbous crop circles overlapped to create the illusion of a body, while long, circular rings protruded from the "body" to resemble legs and

Barbury Castle

On July 17, 1991, an amazingly complex pictogram appeared near Barbury Castle, Wiltshire. Barbury Castle is a hill fort, or a defensive settlement made of earth, that was built during the Iron Age. The pictogram found there had a central ringed area surrounded by three individual rings, all connected with a complicated design of thin lines, giving it a triangular shape. When the formation was discovered, reports of loud roaring sounds and mysterious lights accompanied it, adding to its mystery.

antennae. These crop circles were given names such as "The Spider" and "The Scorpion of Devizes."

Dolphin- or whale-shaped pictograms also appeared. They were more symbolic than the realistic-looking insect ones. These cigar-shaped pictograms sported angled lines that protruded from the top and bottom of the cigar shape, similar to fins, while circular rings decorated each end, looking like a head or a tail.

On July 28, a pictogram appeared in Hampshire, England, that looked like a child's stick figure of a person. Then, on August 18, another pictogram appeared in Wiltshire that looked like a long snake slithering along the ground.

As these new fantastic pictograms emerged, croppies tried to make sense of the symbols. Could the insect pictograms be messages about the environment? Should farmers be using less fertilizer on the croplands in southern England? Interpretations differed depending on the background of the person looking at the crop circle. Dowsers—people who sense water and energy using divination—thought Earth energies were responsible. Meteorologists saw weather as the culprit, and some, including an undercover group from the US Central Intelligence Agency, considered the possibility that

Each small part of a fractal is a copy of the entire fractal, making the geometry of a fractal crop circle especially complex.

extraterrestrial visitors were leaving signposts for others passing through.

Mandelbrot Set

On August 12, in Cambridge, England, a new type of crop circle appeared. This crop circle resembled an insect with its series of interconnected solid circles and a set of smaller circles coming off of it, looking like tiny legs. But scientists knew immediately that it was a fractal, first discovered by French mathematician Benoit Mandelbrot.

Jürgen Krönig, an author and photographer known for taking pictures of the natural world, described it this way: "This [pictogram] involves a mathematical figure of fractal geometry, which could only be created with the help of computers."[3] Because the Mandelbrot Set, as it became known, had appeared near Cambridge University, where Mandelbrot was teaching at the time, many people believed it to be a student prank. However, because the pictogram was created with such precision and skill, many others were unsatisfied with that explanation.

As the 1991 crop circle season drew to a close, there were no accepted explanations for the new types of crop circles. With their mixture of complex symbols, sometimes resembling life on Earth, just who or what was creating them? And what was their purpose?

BENOIT MANDELBROT: Born in Warsaw, Poland, in 1924, Benoit Mandelbrot was known as the father of fractals. In 1980, he developed the Mandelbrot Set, a particular type of fractal. He died in 2010.

Chapter 4

Alien Creations

One popular theory about crop circles is that they are messages from extraterrestrials. Reports of UFOs, such as strange lights, orbs, and small discs, seem to support this theory. In addition, people hear odd sounds and experience other mysterious effects in and around crop circles. Complicated pictograms, rife with symbolic meaning, imply that someone or something intelligent designed them. Many people wonder if this intelligence is from another world.

Mysterious Lights

Over the years, observers have noted mysterious lights that range from large balls of orange light that bounced on a field to smaller bluish-white or pink lights that traveled close to the ground.

Mary Freeman reported experiencing one of these lights on July 13, 1988. As she was driving, she noticed the clouds glowing with a gold-white light that was brighter than the moon. Curious, she watched the light slowly descend. As it hung in the air, a thin beam of light shot out at an angle and touched a field below in Silbury Hill. Two days later, the farmer who owned that field discovered a crop circle in that same spot. It was in the design of a Celtic cross.

In 1990, photographer Steven Alexander filmed a disc-shaped object flying low to the ground above a crop circle near Alton Barnes. "The small blinking

A Celtic cross has a long vertical bar with a shorter cross bar approximately one-third of the way down from the top with a circle around the intersection. A crop circle in this design has a center circle with four other circles arranged at each point of the compass.

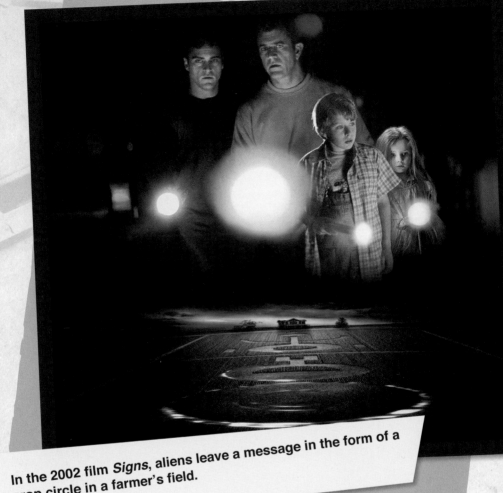

In the 2002 film *Signs*, aliens leave a message in the form of a crop circle in a farmer's field.

object dove into the grain field now and then before it became visible again," said Alexander.[1] The same object then flew past a farmer in a neighboring field, and as it did so, the engine of the farmer's tractor shut off.

In the summer of 1997, aerospace designer Jack Spooncer was driving to his farmhouse in Dorset when he saw a dome of light approximately 200 feet (60 m) in diameter. "There were thousands of points of light, like diamonds, all aligned and geometric," he said. "It was glistening, like a hologram."[2] The next morning, he found two half-ring crop circles stamped into his field.

On August 6, 1999, in the valley of Pewsey, dozens of people saw mysterious lights travel over a field. Some even managed to videotape the event.

Other Effects

In addition to lights, many people have heard strange sounds inside crop circles, such as a low

<u>SIGNS</u>: In 2002, the movie *Signs* premiered. Written and directed by M. Night Shyamalan, the movie stars Mel Gibson. It is about a farm family who discovered a crop circle in their field, which turned out to be a sign that hostile aliens were invading Earth. As a consultant, Colin Andrews provided information about crop circles and acted as a spokesperson with the media.

<u>BALL LIGHTNING</u>: Ball lightning is a phenomenon that occurs during thunderstorms. These glowing spheres appear near the ground, move around, and then disappear, either quietly or with a loud bang. They can be yellow, red, orange, white, or blue, and range in size from tiny to quite large. Often, they have an odor and give off a hissing sound.

humming, similar to high-voltage electric power lines. Others have heard hissing, knocking, or high-pitched whistling sounds. Crackling noises are common and remind people of static electricity. Still others have heard a trilling sound, which many believe is the result of the energy that makes a crop circle. Others attribute this sound to the grasshopper warbler, a bird common in southern England.

The grasshopper warbler has the ability to throw its voice like a ventriloquist, so this bird can fool listeners about its exact location. For this reason, it might be easy to mistake the bird's song for something else entirely.

In addition to sounds, people have experienced headaches when they walk into crop circles that fade away once they leave. They have also experienced nausea and sore throats, tingling sensations, and waves of hot and cold.

Animals are also affected. Dogs sometimes become nervous or violent inside a circle. And dead flies have been found inside crop circles, stuck to the stalks of wheat or other crops. Normally, insecticide would be to blame, but in these cases there were no dead flies on the crops outside the crop circle. Either the farmer only sprayed the crops inside the circle, or something else killed the flies.

People report malfunctions in mechanical and electric equipment. Cameras and cell phones have been known to stop working. Compasses point in the wrong direction. Watches and clocks slow down inside the circle and resume normal operation once they are back outside it. Battery packs become drained of power when set on the ground.

Magnetic Anomalies

One possible explanation for some of these experiences is magnetic anomalies. Starting in the late 1990s, Andrews began measuring Earth's magnetic field in and around crop circles. He found that some crop circles exhibited a higher-than-normal reading as compared to the rest of Earth—some as much as 120 percent more than normal.

TAPE RECORDER: Magnetic tape recorders use a microphone to convert sound waves into electric signals. In turn, these signals go through a recording head, which magnetizes the tape and imprints it with a record of the electric signal.

US scientists William Levengood and John Burke reported high levels of the mineral magnetite inside certain crop circles. Magnetite is a naturally magnetic mineral and often falls to Earth as meteoritic dust. A certain amount of magnetite is found in all soil, approximately 0.4 milligrams per gram, but the concentration of magnetite in crop circles tested by Levengood and Burke ranged from 20 to 250 milligrams per gram. (There are approximately 28 grams in an ounce.) Some people hypothesized that a magnetic field inside crop circles attracted the higher concentrations of magnetite.

The theory proposed that local fluctuations in Earth's magnetic field could create a crop circle and also attract the magnetite. However, scientists believe that local fluctuations would not be strong enough. Another force would be needed to force crops against the ground. The force would need to be an outside horizontal force that would interact with Earth's magnetic field to create a crop circle.

Magnetometers measure the intensity and direction of a magnetic field. Some are designed specifically to measure Earth's magnetic field.

If this outside force exists, is it appearing spontaneously? Or is it created by an intelligent life? Perhaps an alien intelligent life?

The Wessex Triangle

When Andrews first became interested in crop circles, he kept a large map of England in his home office. The map was riddled

Earth's Magnetic Field

Approximately 1,800–3,200 miles (2,900–5,150 km) below the surface of Earth is the planet's outer core, an area filled with iron so hot it is in liquid form. The temperature of this iron is 1,830 degrees Fahrenheit (1,000°C). It surrounds a solid inner core, also made of iron. As the liquid iron flows across the solid iron, a magnetic field is formed. This turns the entire planet into a large bar magnet with two poles—the North and the South Poles.

with multicolored pushpins, which represented all of the crop circles recorded in the area. Andrews tried to find a pattern in the pins, but other than clumps near Stonehenge and Silbury Hill, he could not see one.

On September 4, 1986, Andrews took a soil sample from a crop circle in Wantage. He then left the field at 4:15 p.m. and went home. After dropping the soil sample on his desk near the map, he thought no more about it. That night, at exactly 4:15 a.m., his home security alarm went off. The

The Wessex Triangle

next night, it did it again. The same thing happened every night for 14 days in a row.

Andrews could find no explanation for the faulty alarm. Not only was he an electrical engineer, but he had designed the alarm in his house. If anyone could find the problem, he could.

After being awakened for two weeks straight, Andrews wandered into his office and glanced at the map. Then he noticed it. All the crop circles formed a triangle across three counties, from Oxfordshire to Hampshire to Wiltshire. Andrews measured the distance between each point on the triangle.

The triangle's sides were each 41.5 miles (67 km) long. As soon as he realized the pins formed a triangle, he noticed the alarms had stopped.

This area of England—which became known as the Wessex Triangle—was already known for its high number of UFO sightings. Now it was the center of crop circle activity.

Doubts about the Alien Theory

The alien theory of crop circle formation left many people unsatisfied. If aliens are so technologically advanced that they can travel to our solar system, skeptics wondered, why were they using such a primitive method of communication? Why were the designs so cryptic? And why were they in such rural, isolated communities? If aliens really wanted to communicate with us, they could do so in a more direct way. For instance, why not create a crop circle on the White House lawn?

UFO REPORT: In 2000, the British government issued a 400-page report on UFO sightings. The report concluded there was no evidence of aliens. Instead, the sightings were most likely due to natural events that occurred rarely. Because they were so rare, most people had never seen them before, so they reported them as UFOs.

Chapter 5

Other Explanations

Although the alien theory of crop circle formation is perhaps the most widely known, many other theories attempt to explain crop circles.

A Living Earth

In 1979, scientist James Lovelock introduced the concept that Earth is a living, breathing organism, similar to the human body, called Gaia. Similar to a human body, it has its own form of nerves and blood vessels, such as lakes and rivers. It can also react to changes in the environment just as a human body can. Lovelock called Earth a superorganism.

In addition, many people believe that human bodies have meridians, a type of life artery that flows through the body. When people go in for acupuncture treatment, for instance, they are really getting their meridians balanced. The belief is that unbalanced meridians can lead to sickness and disease. The meridians belonging to Earth are called ley lines, an invisible net of life energy that encompasses the entire planet. Places where ley lines intersect are supposed to be centers of great power and energy.

Over the centuries, it is thought that many cultures built their most sacred sites

JAMES LOVELOCK: While working at NASA during the 1960s, James Lovelock was tasked with studying the atmosphere on Mars. When he compared the lifeless Martian atmosphere to Earth's much more complex atmosphere, he had a revelation. In order for Earth's atmosphere to support life, he believed there must be a control system that included the entire planet and all life on it. He named the theory after Gaia, the Greek goddess of Earth.

GEOMANCY: Geomancy is the practice of trying to foretell the future or discover the unknown. Some use it to discover the location of ley lines. Some practitioners throw rocks or dirt on the ground. Others draw dots on paper and connect them. Practitioners believe the patterns that emerge in either method provide information on whatever is being asked.

Stonehenge

The World Heritage Convention calls Stonehenge the "most architecturally sophisticated prehistoric stone circle in the world."[1] Unlike the hundreds of other stone circles in England, Stonehenge's stones are smooth and uniform. In addition, gigantic horizontal lintels rest atop the large standing stones. English astronomer Gerald S. Hawkins discovered that Stonehenge also acts as a calendar. On the summer solstice, the "heel stone" perfectly aligns with the sun and the altar, which rests in the center of the circle. It is believed that ancient peoples used stone circles similar to Stonehenge to keep track of astronomy so they would know when to plant and harvest their crops, as well as when to have celebrations.

and buildings on these centers of power. These sites include stone markers, earthen walls, pyramids, and churches. Wiltshire County has many sacred sites, including Avebury, Silbury Hill, and Stonehenge. In fact, Stonehenge is supposedly built on an intersection of six ley lines.

The fact that so many crop circles appear in Wiltshire, with its abundance of sacred sites, suggests a connection between crop circles and ley lines. Could it be possible that Gaia is communicating to the human race through the symbols in crop circles? Or could Gaia be reacting to the abuses of pollution and climate change the same way a body reacts to an injury? Could a crop circle be a form of bruise on the living, breathing world in which we live?

Stonehenge is likely a prehistoric sacred site.

The Power of Thought

Some people believe the collective human subconscious is able to control the environment. Since all things humans create begin as thoughts, these theorists believe it is possible that we unconsciously project our thoughts into farm fields and manipulate the plasma vortices that might be creating crop circles.

Another theory involves so-called orgone energy. In the early twentieth century, Austrian physician Wilhelm Reich proposed that a type of energy he called orgone energy controlled everything in Earth's surface, atmosphere, and sea. Therefore, if our collective subconscious has the power to control the environment, as some believe, it can manipulate orgone energy and create crop circles. This could be because we sense the danger from pollution, clear-cutting of rain forests, climate change, and other environmental threats to the planet. Thus, crop circles might be our reaction to this danger.

Dowsing

Dowsing is the perceived ability to detect water, lost objects, hidden information, or energy fields using a divining rod. It is not scientifically proven, but many believe dowsers feel magnetic fields, energy, or other subtle forces that lead them to what they seek. Divining rods are forked sticks made of hazel wood, ash, or rowan. They can also be made of a Y-shaped piece of metal or consist of a pendulum hung from nylon or silk thread. The most common are two rods, one held in each hand, consisting of copper wire bent at right angles. The rods are an L shape, with the short end approximately five inches (13 cm) long and the longer end approximately ten inches (25 cm) long. Dowsers hold the short end of each rod loosely; the other end points out and, together, the two rods indicate where the lost object or water is located.

Relationship to Water

Many crop circles appear near sources of water, such as ponds, aquifers, wells, and underground tanks. Aquifers are large areas of porous rock, sand, or gravel through which water flows underground. Since aquifers enlarge or shrink

Dowsing is a form of divination used to detect energy or find hidden objects.

depending on the amount of rain that has fallen, one theory suggests that this expansion and contraction of the rocks builds up a charge of static electricity. Eventually, the static discharges create a crop circle on the ground above the aquifer. People use the technique of dowsing to try to find underground water as well as ley lines.

Because of climate change and the more extreme weather patterns that seem to be occurring now, the levels of aquifers might be changing more rapidly.

Many crop circles are created by humans, but some are not so easily explained.

This means the static electricity is discharging more often than it had been before the 1970s. This could explain why crop circles began appearing more often in the 1980s and 1990s.

Microwave Energy

Microwave radiation is a type of radiation, or energy, that occurs naturally across Earth. Similar to other forms of radiation, such as X-rays, radio waves, and even the light we see when we turn on a lightbulb, microwaves are in the form of a wave.

Everyday household items emit microwaves, even chairs, pencils, tables, and lamps. Trees, grass, rocks, and soil do as well. When any two items are placed next to each other, their microwaves connect.

When scientists have taken samples of plants from crop circles, they have found that the plants' nodes, or attachment points for leaves, are often swollen or have exploded. Some believe that microwave radiation causes this to happen, which is similar to how microwave ovens cook food. Could microwaves also cause an entire crop circle to form?

An experiment was conducted in which plants were put in a microwave oven on a rotating dish. When the microwave was turned on, the plants laid down, similar to how they lay down in crop circles. However, the plants died, which is not what happens in crop circles. So even though scientists suspect microwave energy affects the nodes of the plants, there is no evidence that it also causes entire crop circles to form.

The Work of Humans

Many people believe humans are to blame for all crop circles. Many creators have confessed. Some consider themselves artists, using the landscape for their canvas. Others enjoy making people fall for their hoaxes. Some farmers might create crop circles and then charge croppies money to walk out to the circles and inspect them. However, some circles cannot be easily explained this way. They are too perfect, and they appear too quickly. Not only do they emerge overnight, but there is often more than one at a time. The man-made circles are generally easy to spot because they are poorly constructed.

Another theory is that governments use satellites to create crop circles. The idea is that a laser is used to make a pictogram. However, nothing seems to be gained economically, militarily, or strategically from making crop circles. In addition, crop circles are known to have appeared before satellites were invented.

Others speculate that military helicopters land in fields and cause crop circles to form with their rotating blades. There is no evidence to support this theory, however.

Doubts about These Theories

The problem with all of these theories is that many of them only explain one part of the crop circle phenomenon. Nor do they offer any proof. For instance, the Gaia theory does not address the fact that many of the pictograms are highly complex and indicate an intelligence behind the design. Neither water nor microwaves could create a complex pictogram. And there is no proof that collective human thought can force crops to lay down in a circle, let alone draw a complicated pictogram.

In addition, none of these theories address other observed phenomena. Just why do so many people see glowing lights in the night sky before a crop circle appears? And why is the magnetic field affected in so many of them?

Hedgehogs

Flying Saucer Review writer Gordon Creighton once remarked sarcastically that mating hedgehogs were creating crop circles. He meant the comment as a criticism of the media, who were printing what he thought were outlandish theories about crop circles and taking them seriously. However, his comment backfired when the media missed his sarcasm and thought hedgehogs were a legitimate suspect in crop circle creation.

Chapter 6

Scientific Investigation

As the crop circle phenomena continued, scientists began studying the plants and soil of crop circles in order to gain a better understanding of how they might be formed. The most extensive investigations were performed by US biophysicist William Levengood.

Plant Anomalies

In December 1990, Levengood became interested in the crop circles that were appearing in England. He contacted Delgado and asked for plant samples to be sent to his Michigan laboratory. He wanted plants both from inside crop circles and from the fields nearby. The

Biophysicist William Levengood theorized that crop circles involve quick heating that affects the size, shape, and future growth of wheat plant cells.

nearby samples would be his control samples, or the standard against which the results of his experiment would be compared. Happy to comply, Delgado sent him wheat and barley from two different crop circles and the nearby fields.

Upon first examination, Levengood noticed that the growth nodes on the crop circle plants were longer and thicker than on the control group. Then

Levengood put the plants under a microscope. There he saw that the cell wall pits were also enlarged. Cell wall pits are tiny ducts or depressions where cells exchange fluids and matter with other cells.

The optical microscope uses glass lenses to enlarge an image. Simple microscopes have one lens and magnify by 300 percent. Compound microscopes have multiple lenses and magnify up to 2,000 percent.

What could cause this enlargement of the cell wall pits? Levengood theorized that a quick heating of the fluids inside the plants could be to blame, so he set up a small experiment in a microwave oven. He put plants in the oven and turned it on. Afterward, he examined the plants and found the same enlargement of the cell wall pits. This supported his theory that some sort of quick heating had affected the plants in the crop circles.

In addition, Levengood looked at the seeds of the plants. The crop circle plants had smaller seeds than the control plants, and sometimes no seeds were present at all. When he tried to germinate, or grow, the seeds, he found the crop circle seeds did not develop normally. Sometimes there was no growth, and other times there was less growth than normal.

MICROWAVE OVEN: Microwave ovens use high-frequency microwaves, a form of electromagnetic radiation, to cook food. Water, fat, sugars, and other molecules absorb the microwaves, which then vibrate and emit a large amount of heat.

The BLT Investigation

With these promising results, Levengood teamed up with two other people and formed BLT in 1992. BLT stands for John Burke, William Levengood, and Nancy Talbott. Burke was a New York businessman with an avid interest in science. Talbott was a record producer with a history of academic research. Levengood was the scientist who led the investigations.

Over the years, the BLT group investigated crop circle plants. Talbott set up a system for obtaining crop circle samples from all over the world as well as rules for obtaining the samples from the field so that all the samples would be taken the same way. She made sure the samples would be random, and she

A farmer looks for wheat stalks with unusual nodes in a crop circle in his field.

trained new personnel to assist in gathering samples. She also found funding for the research.

Burke assisted Levengood with experiments and conducted research related to Levengood's results. He made sure to be aware of all new crop circle research being performed.

Eventually BLT expanded to include several hundred field personnel in Europe, the United States, and Canada. In addition, it employed consultants from many different disciplines, including geology, chemistry, physics, mineralogy, and astronomy.

Long-Term Results

After eight years of research, BLT had collected more than 300 samples of crops from the United States, Canada, and several countries in Europe. The plants studied came from simple crop circles as well as complex pictograms. The study noted the following irregularities:

- Cell wall pits were enlarged.
- Stem nodes were longer and thicker by 30–200 percent more than normal.
- Growth nodes were bent at a 10- to 90-degree angle, usually on the last node or the second-to-last node.
- Growth nodes showed signs of bursting open.
- Seed heads were either smaller than normal or had missing seeds.
- Seeds grew slower or did not grow at all in laboratory conditions.
- Anomalies were more pronounced closer to the center of the crop circle.

Study Criticisms

One of the criticisms of BLT's work is that the investigations were not conducted in the form of a blind study. A blind study is one in which the investigators do not know whether they are testing a control group or not. In the case of crop circles, a blind study would hide whether a plant sample came from inside a crop circle or from the nearby fields. The purpose of a blind study is to eliminate bias.

Andrews formulated a blind test using BLT's own sampling team. His test found Levengood's results to be flawed or misinterpreted.

Man-Made Crop Circles

Plants from known man-made crop circles were also studied. Levengood found that the plants from the man-made circles did not include the same anomalies as the other ones he had been studying. Some of them had slightly enlarged nodes, but none of the other anomalies existed.

This led Levengood to conduct an experiment of his own on man-made crop circles in 1997. He wanted to see how fertilizer and ripeness would affect his results. In Maryland, he had three sets of crop circles created in wheat fields. The first set was made on June 3, the second on June 13, and the third on July 25. Each set consisted of two fertilized and two non-fertilized crop circles.

After taking samples from all three sets, Levengood found that the nodes of the plants inside the crop circles were approximately 10 percent longer than the plants outside the crop circles. Levengood believed that the increased node size was a result of geotropic reaction, or the plants' natural inclination to become vertical again. Fertilizer had no effect on the results.

Like the other man-made crop circles, the plants in Levengood's circles showed no signs of any other anomalies. This implied that something else was affecting plants inside mystery crop circles, something other than the bending that also occurs in man-made crop circles.

Similar to Terrence Meaden, Levengood liked the idea that plasma vortices were creating crop circles. He even wrote a scientific paper that expanded on Meaden's theory. Plasma vortices remain an unproven theory.

GEOTROPIC REACTION: Tropism is the natural reaction of a plant or animal to a stimulus, such as gravity, light, water, chemicals, or something mechanical. Geotropism is when plants react to gravity, such as when roots grow downward and the plant itself grows upward.

Chapter 7

Forgers Come Forward

As theories circulated about who or what was making crop circles and what message they might be sending to the human race, an answer soon burst upon the scene. It was an answer that devastated cereologists, croppies, and those hoping to find a deeper meaning to crop circles.

Hoaxers

On September 9, 1991, a headline appeared in the British newspaper *Today* that read "The Men Who Conned the World." The article detailed how retirees Doug Bower and Dave Chorley, while spending a boring evening in a pub, had come up with the idea of fooling people into thinking UFOs had landed in the fields near where they lived.

Without informing their wives, Bower and Chorley would sneak out of their houses in the middle of the night and make crop circles using simple tools. Their scheme worked so well that they continued to improve their designs over the years, enjoying the reactions from croppies.

"We just wanted people to think that a UFO had landed in a field, when it was really just two blokes with a plank of wood," said Bower, years later. "We'd make the crop circles and crowds would come to see them. We used to mingle with them and listen to what they were saying, all these so-called

Cereology is the study of crop circles, and cereologists are those who study them. The name is based on Ceres, the ancient Roman goddess of agriculture.

UFO experts spouting off about aliens. We would look at each other and burst out laughing."[1]

Why had they suddenly decided to come clean in 1991, so many years after the phenomenon captured the world's interest? Bower was 67 and Chorley was 62, and they both felt they were getting too old to go stomping through fields every night. They were feeling guilty about lying to their wives. And they had heard the British government

To bend the crops, many circle makers use a "stalk stomper," a simple plank with a rope attached.

was going to invest money in crop circle research, which they thought could be better spent on more important things.

Doubt about the Hoaxers

The public and the media latched onto Bower and Chorley's claims, but many people were skeptical. For one thing, how had they made the tiny grapeshot crop circles that were not connected to anything else? Bower and Chorley claimed they jumped to the grapeshots from a tramline, but in order to do that, they would have had to travel 35 feet (11 m) in some instances.

In addition, Bower and Chorley said they used a baseball cap with a metal frame attached in order to draw straight lines. However, many were skeptical that the homemade contraption was capable of drawing the perfectly straight lines that appeared in the pictograms. There was doubt that their wives would not have noticed them sneaking out in the middle of the night for so many years, often every single night in a row for months on end during the summer. Finally, Bower and Chorley stated they had stayed in a small region of England. Crop circles appeared all over the world during this time.

Other Hoaxers

The most likely explanation for the holes in Bower and Chorley's story is that they were lying about some parts of it. As other hoaxers came forward in the 1990s, it became clear that many different groups were involved in making the circles.

For instance, in the early 1990s, a group known as the United Bureau of Investigation created crop circles because they hoped it would help them contact extraterrestrials. And by 1999, Joachim Koch and Hans-Jürgen Kyborg had made nine crop circles in Alton Barnes. Like the United Bureau of Investigation, Koch and Kyborg wanted to contact extraterrestrials. They hoped their crop circles would send a message to the intelligent life they believed had created the mystery crop circles.

Mathematical Ratios

In 1992, astronomer Gerald S. Hawkins began looking for patterns in the measurements of crop circles, specifically those with more than one circle or ring. He found that many crop circles had ratios that matched the diatonic scale. The diatonic scale is a musical octave consisting of eight notes, such as the eight white notes on a piano. Not only that, Hawkins found that other geometric ratios existed among crop circle measurements. For the hoaxers to be able to make crop circles exhibiting these precise ratios, without being mathematicians themselves, seemed doubtful to Hawkins.

Crop Circle Contest

On the evening of July 11, 1992, the International Crop Circle Making Competition was held for the first and only time. Twelve teams signed up to create identical crop circles during the night. The best-looking crop circle would win £3,000 (approximately $6,000 at the time). Media covered the event.

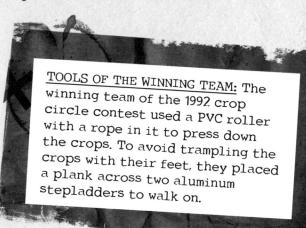

TOOLS OF THE WINNING TEAM: The winning team of the 1992 crop circle contest used a PVC roller with a rope in it to press down the crops. To avoid trampling the crops with their feet, they placed a plank across two aluminum stepladders to walk on.

After the teams worked all night, photographs were taken of the completed crop circles from a helicopter the next morning. "When we flew around the hill of West Wycombe, an unforgettable sight greeted us," said John Macnish, a documentary film producer. "In the golden wheat beneath us, 12 practically identical pictograms were stretched out along the tractor [tramlines]."[2] The contest proved people could create complicated pictograms using simple tools in just one night.

Groups of artist-hoaxers create crop circles all over the world.

Proof

Even though Bower and Chorley's claims seemed farfetched to many, Andrews received proof of their claims in the mid-1990s. A BBC reporter told Andrews he had been following Bower and Chorley around for two years, filming them as they made crop circles. They had even created a crop circle as a present for the reporter's son's birthday. In addition, Bower and Chorley had sketched their designs on the back of envelopes. They then pasted a stamp on the envelopes and mailed them to themselves so they would be postmarked with an exact date. The envelopes contained information on when and where the particular designs would appear.

Since Andrews had been keeping a database of all crop circles as part of his ongoing investigation, he was able to verify that these designs had indeed appeared at these locations on those dates. Bower and Chorley had provided undeniable proof that they had successfully hoaxed people for 13 years.

As to Bower and Chorley's claim that they had made all of the crop circles, the reporter had evidence proving that was not true. He had filmed other hoaxers during the time he had filmed Bower and Chorley.

Investigating the Man-Made Circles

After seeing proof of hoaxing, Andrews began his own investigation during 1999 and 2000. He wanted to see if there was a difference between crop circles that were known to be man-made and those as yet unexplained. After all, crop circles had been spotted

ALIEN INVADERS: In 1967, two British college students created six egg-shaped metallic spacecraft as a hoax and planted them around England. In each spacecraft, they installed a speaker that emitted a wailing noise. They also inserted an old smelly piece of bread dough intended to look like alien brains. The hoax fooled the public, the media, and even British intelligence agents.

for possibly hundreds of years before Bower and Chorley were even born. And since Bower and Chorley's retirement, the crop circles continued to appear. Were they all from hoaxers? Could some of these crop circles be from nonhuman sources?

During the late 1990s, newspapers, radio, and television stations often hired people to create crop circles. Andrews asked his media contacts to tell him when and where these man-made crop circles would appear. He also engaged former police detectives and private detectives to follow suspected hoaxers and to infiltrate the hoaxing teams. Then he traveled to the sites and inspected the crop circles, comparing them to other crop circles that were not known to be man-made.

In the man-made circles, he often found evidence of human intervention, such as walking paths and holes used for stakes. In addition, when Andrews took readings of magnetic fields within the man-made circles, he did not find any anomalies. Curiously enough, this lack of anomalies was always true in the more complex pictograms. In the simplest circles, the kind that had been around for hundreds of years, he continued to find anomalies.

When Andrews tallied his data, he discovered that approximately 20 percent of crop circles from 1999 through 2000 had these anomalies. These were the simplest circles, and he thought they were legitimate. The rest, which were the most complex, did not have these anomalies. Therefore he concluded they were man-made.

How to Make a Crop Circle

1. Ask the farmer for permission.
2. Create a center point by stomping down crops in a circle.
3. Trample a line to the outer rim with your plank, or "stalk stomper."
4. As a partner holds a piece of rope in the center point, walk around the edge, stomping down crops and holding the rope tight.
5. After the edge is complete, trample down the inside with your plank.

Chapter 8

Cereal Art

After the hoaxers came forward in 1991, crop circles continued to appear throughout England and the rest of the world. Hoaxers usually did not admit to making particular designs, and many croppies still believed that most crop circles were the real deal, created by aliens or Earth's energy or some other source yet to be discovered. However, no matter what agent they believed created the crop circles, few could dispute their beauty. Crop circles had become an art form, appearing as DNA structures, helixes, webs, knots, and complex geometric patterns.

The Artists

John Lundberg of Circlemakers certainly believes he and his team are creating art. By day, they are well-paid commercial artists, creating crop advertisements for recording artists or cell phone companies. By night, they are covert crop circle makers, sneaking into fields and making elaborate pictograms that bring croppies to southern England to view their amazing images.

"We weren't pushing paint around on a canvas that sat in a sterile environment; we were quite literally forming and shaping the culture that surrounds us."[2]
—John Lundberg talking about crop circles, 2009

It is hard work, too, especially the images they make at night. A crop circle usually takes a week to go from the initial design to a completed crop circle. First Lundberg and his team have to make detailed construction drawings on a computer, including all the measurements. Then they choose a location near a hill so the crop circle can be easily seen in the daytime. Finally, they go into the field with a team of people and their tools, minus any flashlights in order to avoid discovery. By morning, the design is complete.

Lundberg and his team try to "use art to perpetuate the mystery and the mythology of crop circles."[1] That is why they do not claim credit for the approximately 70 crop circles they create every year

Doug Bower, the famous crop circle prankster, displays some of his blueprints.

(out of 250 worldwide). Lundberg considers Doug Bower, of the Bower and Chorley team of hoaxers, to be a great artist.

Rob Irving, another crop circle artist, agrees. Bower is "the greatest artist of the twentieth century," he said, "or the most provocative."[3] Irving became interested in crop circles in 1990 and 1991 when he heard someone say crop circles could not possibly be made by humans. Sensing a challenge, he tried to make his own. His first few attempts were clumsy, but soon, croppies were studying his designs as examples of authentic crop circles.

Similar to Lundberg, Irving does some commercial crop circles during the day, but he likes to keep his nighttime circles secret. The art, in the case of crop circles, is not about the artist, he believes. Crop circles are about the mystery and the effect they can have on people.

FIBONACCI SEQUENCE: In 1202, Leonardo Pisano, known as Fibonacci, described a sequence of numbers: 1, 1, 2, 3, 5, 8, 13, 21, etc. Except for the first number, each number is a sum of the two numbers preceding it. This sequence goes on to infinity.

The Fractals

A common theme among pictograms is the fractal. On July 7, 1996, the Julia Set appeared near Stonehenge in Wiltshire. This fractal spiraled out from a large center circle to ever smaller circles, each one a smaller copy of the one before it. The way the circles diminished in size followed a particular pattern known as the Fibonacci Sequence.

The Julia Set encompassed 151 circles and measured 915 feet (279 m) along the length of its curve. More than 10,000 visitors came to see it, marveling not just at the design but at the story of how it had appeared, supposedly in a matter of minutes. A pilot flew over the field near Stonehenge at approximately 5:15 p.m. and reported that he did not see anything unusual, but when he flew back at approximately 6:00 p.m., the Julia Set had appeared.

Another type of fractal appeared in 1997— the Koch Snowflake. Developed by a Swedish mathematician in the early twentieth century, the Koch Snowflake is a simpler fractal than the Julia

Snowflake crop circle design

or Mandelbrot Sets, which are impossible to draw without a computer. The Koch Snowflake, however, can be drawn on paper before the repetitions of the design become too small to see.

The first Koch Snowflake appeared close to Silbury Hill and set a record for the amount of grain flattened in a single crop circle: 0.86 acres (0.34 ha). The second snowflake appeared on Milk Hill near Alton Barnes. This one had one snowflake inside another, making it look as if it were inside out.

The Universe

Another common theme among crop circle makers was the pictograms that represented suns, moons, stars, and planets.

In Bishops Sutton in 1995, a formation appeared that looks like a series of bubbles of varying sizes, arranged in a ring. The pictogram was actually a representation of an asteroid belt, complete with 99 asteroids.

ASTEROID BELT: Asteroids are rocky bodies that orbit the sun, usually in a flat ring or belt. Most of the millions of asteroids in our solar system are the size of a boulder; at least 30 are more than 125 miles (200 km) in diameter and are considered minor planets.

In 1999, Britain experienced a full solar eclipse.

That summer, a representation of the eclipse appeared in Middle Wallop in a yellow field of oilseed rape, the plant from which canola oil is made. In this pictogram, nine separate images showed the entire progression of a solar eclipse. The yellow of the field seemed particularly appropriate for a representation of a solar eclipse.

One of the most elaborate pictograms ever made appeared near Stanton Saint Bernard in 2001. It consisted of 409 distinct circles arranged

Mayan Calendar

Many people believe there is a correlation between the ancient Mayan calendar and crop circles. For instance, in 1997, a crop circle appeared in Etchilhampton, Wiltshire, that had a grid of 780 squares. A cycle, called a Tzolkin in the ancient Mayan calendar, consists of 260 days, which is one-third of 780. Another example occurred in 1998, when a formation of 52 circles appeared in Beckhampton, Wiltshire. In the Mayan calendar, a "calendar round" is a cycle of 52 years.

It is possible to find crop circles that match nearly all of the known cycles in the Mayan calendar.

in six separate spiral arms, all connected in a giant pinwheel. Each spiral had 13 circles, creating a representation of the galaxy.

Cultural Symbols

Signs and symbols of various cultures have also been represented in pictograms. In June 2001, the sun rose precisely over the apex of the Great Pyramid in Giza, Egypt. Then, a similar pictogram appeared in Alton Barnes. This pictogram showed a pyramid with a sunburst peeking over the apex, just the way it had in Egypt.

In Highclere in 2002, another pyramid appeared in a wheat field. This one was a symbol of the Freemasons, a secret society that is more than 200 years old. In this pictogram, a large eye sat in the apex of the pyramid with a sunburst surrounding it. The entire image was enclosed in a ring. The eye is the Freemason's symbol of an all-seeing God.

The Freemason's pyramid symbol appears on the back of the one-dollar bill.

In addition, several mandala shapes have appeared as crop circles over the years. A mandala, which means "circle" in the Sanskrit language, is often a circle set inside a square. A more complicated mandala showed up in Barbury Castle in 2003. It looks like six daisies intertwined, their petals overlapping each other. However, the mandala is actually a geometric design used in the Buddhist and Hindu religions. Several other mandala crop circles have appeared throughout the years.

The Mandala

In Hinduism and Buddhism, the mandala is a symbol of the universe, a holy place for the gods, and a container of universal forces. To meditate with a mandala, people seek to mentally enter the mandala and follow its twisted paths to the center.

YGGDRASIL: In Norse mythology, Yggdrasil is the name of the World Tree, a giant ash tree that is the source of new life and also supports the universe. One set of its roots goes down to the underworld, another goes to the land of giants, and a third goes to the home of the gods.

A fruit tree with an extensive root system appeared in Alton Barnes in 2002. Many believed this to represent Yggdrasil, also known as the World Tree, from Norse mythology. From one angle, it resembles a fruit tree, but upside down, the roots look like the top of a mushroom and the branches look like the roots of the mushroom.

Man-made images such as this dragonfly do not possess the same patterns or magnetic anomalies as mystery crop circles.

charging for parking, ladders (to see the crop circle from a higher vantage point), soft drinks, and snacks.

Over the years, other crop circles have appeared throughout the world, often reflecting the culture of the country. In the United States, they are often found near Native American sacred sites and appear in fields of soybeans and corn. The circles themselves are less sophisticated than their European counterparts. They usually resemble the early pictograms from England, exemplified by a series of circles connected by thin lines that appeared in Wisconsin in 2003. European mainland crop circles often appear near megaliths, in much the same way crop circles do in England.

Tourism Industry

In southern England, where the crop circle phenomenon began in the 1970s, crop circles have become a big tourist industry. The Barge Inn near Pewsey is iconic among croppies and circle makers alike. For 20 years, people have been coming to the Barge Inn to discuss the latest crop circles. The back room has photographs of crop circles on the ceiling and a bulletin board with information on the latest circles.

In addition to the Barge Inn, it is estimated that Wiltshire's tourist industry brings in millions of pounds each year due to crop circles. Farmers can make thousands of pounds from companies who want their logo pressed into a field, as well as from the tourists who want to step into the fields and examine crop circles up close. People also make money from magazines, calendars, books, and conferences about crop circles. Even a simple photograph can command a high price. "A good aerial picture of a sophisticated circle picked up by the TV or the press can make thousands of pounds," said a man in charge of a picture agency.[2]

Crop Circles Around the World

Country	Number of Crop Circles, 1960–2002
United Kingdom	1,784
United States	228
Canada	135
Germany	105
Austria	71
The Netherlands	62
Hungary	23
Japan	19
France	13
New Zealand	7
Russia	6
Israel	6
Mexico	5
India	4
China	2

EARTH HOUSE: In 2011, Jolson Architecture designed a house that looked like it was sitting next to a series of crop circles. Situated in Australia, this 4-bedroom, rammed-earth house features an entrance that has sculpted concentric circles formed into the landscaping, along with a labyrinth. From above, the landscaping looks like crop circles.

Debate Continues

Today, many people still debate whether crop circles are merely man-made hoaxes or artwork, whether they come from aliens or from human thoughts, or whether they were created by Earth's energy or plasma vortices. Some choose to look at the evidence of hoaxing and say that all but the simplest—or even all circles—are hoaxes. Others look at the evidence Levengood found in plants and dismiss it as faulty research. Still others declare that all circles are important no matter how they were created because they force us to look at our environment and question how we are treating the planet.

"What does this mean?" asked Francine Blake, who founded the Wiltshire crop circle study group in 1995. "It means that we have to take note; something extraordinary is happening. Crop circles are not normal occurrences; they do not fit well with our usual beliefs. This of course is not to everyone's liking—it is not easy to face the unknown."[3]

Crop circles continue to delight and mystify viewers in Wiltshire and around the world.

Tools and Clues

compass— When placed in a crop circle, the needle often swings erratically and then refuses to point north after being removed from the crop circle.

crop circle equipment— A camera, tripod, compass, stepladder, and a tape measure allow investigators to take pictures and record data about crop circles.

crop circle-making tools— The winners of the 1992 crop circle contest used a PVC roller with a rope in it as well as ladder and two planks, which allowed them to walk on the plants without leaving footprints.

divining rods— Dowsers use these wooden or metal Y-shaped rods to locate water, lost objects, or energy fields.

Bower and Chorley's tools— Doug Bower and Dave Chorley used a plank with a rope attached to it as well as a baseball cap covered in a wire contraption in order to make crop circles.

<u>infrared camera–</u>	This allows people to see even in complete darkness.
<u>magnetometer–</u>	Colin Andrews used this to record the magnetic field inside crop circles.
<u>microscope–</u>	William Levengood used a microscope to examine anomalies in plants that come from within crop circles and compare them to the plants from nearby fields.
<u>microwave oven–</u>	Levengood heated plants in a microwave to see if high-intensity heat could cause them to lay down as they do in crop circles. However, the plants died after laying down, which is not what happens in crop circles.
<u>night vision goggles–</u>	These magnify low levels of light so investigators can see crop circles at night.
<u>ultralight planes–</u>	These light airplanes are flown over crop circles to give a better view of the overall design of a crop circle.

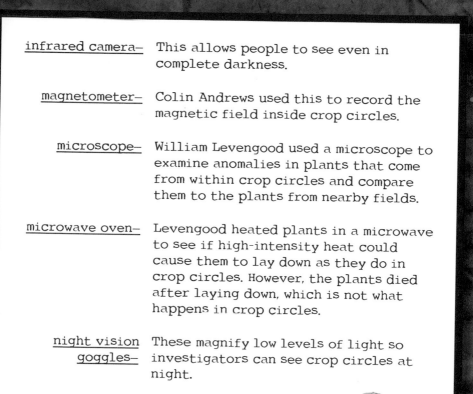

Timeline

1678   On August 22, an account of a devil flattening a field of oats near Hertfordshire is printed in a pamphlet, along with a woodcut illustrating the event.

1880   A letter written by John Rand Capron about crops being flattened into a circular shape is printed in the journal *Nature*. He attributes this phenomenon to a whirlwind or a cyclone.

1920s   Young Roger Sear explores "witch's rings" and experiences strange phenomena.

1935   A ten-year-old boy and an adult witness a crop circle form from a whirlwind.

1943   A pilot in the British air force takes aerial photographs of a crop circle in Sussex, England.

1972   On August 15, two men report witnessing a crop circle form in front of them in England.

1979	Scientist James Lovelock develops the theory that Earth is a living, breathing superorganism.
1980	Meteorologist Terrence Meaden hypothesizes that crop circles are formed by stationary whirlwinds.
1981	During the summer, Patrick Delgado witnesses his first crop circle in Cheesefoot Head. He alerts local newspapers, as well as the BBC and ITN.
1983	In July, Colin Andrews sees his first crop circles and begins investigating the phenomenon.
1985	Amateur pilot Busty Taylor teams up with Andrews and Delgado to survey crop circles from the air.
1985	Andrews, Delgado, and Taylor form Circles Phenomenon Research International.
1986	Andrews notices that many of the crop circles in southern England are grouped together in a triangle that becomes known as the Wessex Triangle, an area known for UFO sightings.
1989	Delgado and Andrews write the first book about crop circles, *Circular Evidence*.
1989	Operation White Crow is created to witness a crop circle as it forms. After a week, the operation breaks up due to lack of evidence.
1990	In April, the Center for Crop Circle Studies is formed to study crop circles free of bias.
1990	On May 23, the first pictogram appears near Cheesefoot Head, England, below Telegraph Hill.

Timeline

1990   In late July, Delgado and Andrews stage Operation Blackbird in order to spot a crop circle being formed. The operation ends when they are fooled by a fake crop circle made by hoaxers.

1990   In December, William Levengood begins examining crop circle plants and comparing them to control plants in nearby fields.

1991   From June through August, pictograms resembling insects, dolphins, and humans begin appearing in southern England.

1991   On August 12, the Mandelbrot Set appears in Cambridge, England. It is the first completely recognizable pictogram.

1991   On September 9, Doug Bower and Dave Chorley announce they have been creating crop circles for 13 years to fool people into believing that UFOs had landed in England.

<u>1992</u>	On July 11, a crop circle competition is held in which 12 teams compete to create a specific design. All of the teams are able to recreate the design overnight using primitive tools.
<u>1992</u>	Mathematician Gerald S. Hawkins discovers that many crop circles are made with an exact diatonic ratio, as well as other geometric ratios.

<u>MID-1990s</u>	Andrews receives proof from a BBC reporter that Bower and Chorley, as well as other hoaxers, had made many of the crop circles they claimed to have made.
<u>1997</u>	Another fractal known as the Koch Snowflake appears in two places in Wiltshire. The first of them breaks records for the amount of grain flattened in a single design.
<u>1997</u>	Levengood experiments with plants from man-made crop circles. He does not find the same anomalies in them that he finds in the crop circle plants.
<u>1999-2000</u>	Andrews measures the magnetic fields in known man-made crop circles and compares them to others of unknown origin. It is concluded during the two-year investigation that approximately 80 percent of crop circles in England are man-made.
<u>LATE 1990s-PRESENT DAY</u>	Crop circles continue to appear all over the world with complex designs such as geometric figures, mazes, forms of life, the universe, knots, fractals, and others.

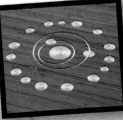

Glossary

anomaly . . . . Irregularity or variance.

barrow . . . . Burial mound.

cereal . . . . Any plant of the grass family that produces an edible grain, including oats, barley, rye, wheat, rice, and corn.

extraterrestrial . . . Existing or coming from somewhere outside of Earth.

fractal . . . . A geometric shape that can be repeatedly subdivided, each subdivision of which is a smaller copy of the whole.

hoax . . . . An act intended to trick people.

lintel . . . . A horizontal piece of stone or wood set over an opening.

magnetic field..... An area surrounding a magnetic body in
which the magnetic force is felt.

megalith .... An enormous stone, usually standing
upright or forming part of a prehistoric
structure.

node .... A point on a plant where a leaf meets
the stem.

pictogram .... An image that gains meaning through its
resemblance to a physical object.

plasma .... A hot, ionized gas made up of ions and
electrons.

surveillance ...... Continual observance of a person, group,
or place.

vortex .... A whirling mass of something, especially
water or air, that draws everything near
its center.

Additional Resources

Selected Bibliography

Alexander, Steven, and Karen Alexander. *Crop Circles: Signs, Wonders and Mysteries.* London: Arcturus, 2006. Print.

Anderhub, Werner, and Hans Peter Roth. *Crop Circles: Exploring the Designs & Mysteries.* New York: Lark, 2002. Print.

Andrews, Colin, and Stephen J. Spignesi. *Crop Circles: Signs of Contact.* Franklin Lakes, New Jersey: New Page, 2003. Print.

Haselhoff, Eltjo. *The Deepening Complexity of Crop Circles: Scientific Research and Urban Legends.* Berkeley, California: Frog, 2001. Print.

Silva, Freddy. *Secrets in the Fields: The Science and Mysticism of Crop Circles.* Charlottesville, VA: Hampton Roads, 2002. Print.

Further Readings

Burns, Jan. *Crop Circles: Mysterious Encounters.* New Haven: KidHaven, 2008. Print.

Pringle, Lucy. *Crop Circles: Art in the Landscape.* London: Frances Lincoln Limited, 2007.

Web Links

To learn more about crop circles, visit ABDO Publishing Company online at **www.abdopublishing.com**. Web sites about crop circles are featured on our Book Links page. These links are routinely monitored and updated to provide the most current information available.

Places to Visit

Avebury

Located in Avebury, 7 miles (11.3 km) west of Marlborough, Wiltshire, England

44-0-1672-539-250

http://www.english-heritage.org.uk/daysout/properties/avebury

After Stonehenge, Avebury is the second-most impressive megalith in England. While there, visit Silbury Hill, the largest man-made mound in the world.

Bratton Camp and White Horse

Located 2 miles (3.2 km) east of Westbury off B3098, 1 mile (1.6 km) southwest of Bratton, Wiltshire, England

http://www.english-heritage.org.uk/daysout/properties/bratton-camp-and-white-horse

Bratton Camp, or Castle, is a hill fort dating back to the Iron Age. A large white drawing of a horse decorates one side of the fort.

Stonehenge

Located off A344 Road, Amesbury, Wiltshire, England

44-0-870-333-1181

http://www.english-heritage.org.uk/stonehenge

Stonehenge is the most spectacular and iconic megalith in all of England. These standing stones date back to prehistoric times.

Source Notes

Chapter 1. Mysterious Discoveries

1. Werner Anderhub and Hans Peter Roth. *Crop Circles: Exploring the Designs & Mysteries.* New York: Lark, 2002. Print. 13.

2. Ibid. 16.

3. "Crop Circles: Artworks or Alien Signs?" *National Geographic News.* National Geographic Society, 2 Aug. 2002. Web. 2 Aug. 2011.

Chapter 2. Early Sightings

1. Andy Thomas. *Vital Signs: A Complete Guide to the Crop Circle Mystery and Why It Is Not a Hoax.* Berkeley, CA: Frog, 1998. Print. 32.

2. Colin Andrews. *Crop Circles: Signs of Contact.* Franklin Lakes, NJ: New Page, 2003. Print. 40.

3. "The Helions Bumpstead Circles." *Old Crop Circles.* Old Crop Circles, 2011. Web. 2 Aug. 2011.

4. Werner Anderhub and Hans Peter Roth. *Crop Circles: Exploring the Designs & Mysteries.* New York: Lark, 2002. Print. 23.

5. Pat Delgado and Colin Andrews. *Circular Evidence.* London: Bloomsbury, 1989. Print. 21.

Chapter 3. Complicated Designs

1. Werner Anderhub and Hans Peter Roth. *Crop Circles: Exploring the Designs & Mysteries.* New York: Lark, 2002. Print. 26.

2. Ibid. 27.

3. Ibid. 28.

Chapter 4. Alien Creations

1. Werner Anderhub and Hans Peter Roth. *Crop Circles: Exploring the Designs & Mysteries.* New York: Lark, 2002. Print. 113.

2. Freddy Silva, *Secrets in the Fields: The Science and Mysticism of Crop Circles.* Charlottesville, VA: Hampton Roads, 2002. Print. 137.

Chapter 5. Other Explanations

1. "Stonehenge, Avebury and Associated Sites." *United Nations Educational, Scientific, and Cultural Organization.* UNESCO World Heritage Centre, 2011. Web. 2 Aug. 2011.

Chapter 6. Scientific Investigation

None.

Chapter 7. Forgers Come Forward

1. David Harrison "The Fellowship of the Rings." *Daily Telegraph.* 25 July 2004. *circlemakers.org.* Circlemakers.org, n.d. Web. 2 Aug. 2011.

2. Werner Anderhub and Hans Peter Roth. *Crop Circles: Exploring the Designs & Mysteries.* New York: Lark, 2002. Print. 106.

Chapter 8. <u>Cereal Art</u>

1. David Harrison "The Fellowship of the Rings." *Daily Telegraph*. 25 July 2004. *circlemakers.org*. Circlemakers.org, n.d. Web. 2 Aug. 2011.

2. "Crop Circles: Artworks or Alien Signs?" *National Geographic News*. National Geographic Society, 2 Aug. 2002. Web. 2 Aug. 2011.

3. David Jenkins. "Crop Circle Conundrum." *Telegraph*. Telegraph Media Company, 25 Aug. 2010. Web. 2 Aug. 2011.

Chapter 9. <u>Crop Circles Today</u>

1. Lee Speigel. "Crop Circle Found in Indonesia Rice Field." *AOL News*. AOL News, 24 Jan. 2011. Web. 2 Aug. 2011.

2. John Vidal. "The Bizarre Revival of Crop Circles—and Advice on How to Make Your Own." *guardian.co.uk*. Guardian News and Media, 5 June 2009. Web. 2 Aug. 2011.

3. Ibid.

Index

Index
Continued

About the Author

Andrea Pelleschi has been writing and editing children's books for more than 12 years, including storybooks, novelty books, fiction, and nonfiction. She has a Master of Fine Arts degree in creative writing from Emerson College and has taught writing classes for college freshmen.

About the Content Consultant

Colin Andrews is an internationally renowned author and researcher. He is an engineer by profession and was a principle official in British Regional Government. He coined the term *crop circles* while advising Queen Elizabeth II. He holds the most extensive database of crop circle information in the world.

Photo Credits

Robert Harding Travel/Photolibrary, cover, 3; Peter Mukherjee/ iStockphoto, 7; Troy Maben/AP Images, 9, 96 (bottom); Nancy Nehring/ iStockphoto, 11, 96 (top); Joze Pojbic/iStockphoto, 14, 101 (bottom); The British Library/Photolibrary, 17; Dzianis Miraniuk/Bigstock, 19; Frank Masi/Paramount Pictures/Photofest, 21; Colin Andrews/www. ColinAndrews.net, 24, 33, 99; iStockphoto, 35, 95, 105; English Heritage/Photolibrary, 38; John Scott/iStockphoto, 41; Buena Vista Pictures/Photofest, 42; Andrew Howe/iStockphoto, 44; John A. Bone/ AP Images, 46, 97; Red Line Editorial, 48; Bryan Busovicki/Bigstock, 53; Peter Titmuss/Alamy, 55; Matteo Gamba/Fotolia, 56, 98; Gustav Bergman/iStockphoto, 59; Tammy McAllister/Bigstock, 61, 100; Wavebreak Media Ltd./Bigstock, 62; Susan Tusa/AP Images, 64, 101 (top); Carol M. Highsmith's America/Library of Congress, 69; Trinity Mirror/Mirrorpix/Alamy, 70, 81; Daily Mail/Rex/Alamy, 74; Klas Stolpe/AP Images, 79; English Heritage.NMR/Heritage-Images, 83; David Pedre/iStockphoto, 85; Makaule/Bigstock, 86; Godong Godong/ Photolibrary, 87; Jack Barker/Alamy, 89; AP Images, 91